Totline®

SOCIAL SKILLS

Play & Learn Pages
with ideas for parents and kids to share

American Education Publishing™
An imprint of Carson-Dellosa Publishing LLC
Greensboro, North Carolina

American Education Publishing™
An imprint of Carson-Dellosa Publishing LLC
P.O. Box 35665
Greensboro, NC 27425 USA

ISBN 978-1-60996-988-2

01-121127784

TABLE OF CONTENTS

Your Child's DEVELOPING SKILLS

Working and Playing With Others

Parents often view the development of strong academic skills as the single most important thing they can do for their child. In fact, helping your child develop the social skills necessary for success in school is equally important. Social and emotional understanding helps form a strong foundation for success throughout the elementary school years, and even in life. You can prepare your child for school success by helping him or her learn to work and play with others. Focus on these important areas.

Self-Concept

When your child has a good self-concept, he or she will be more likely to confront the challenges of school with confidence and excitement. At the ages of 4–6, many children crave independence and demonstrate a growing ability to take care of themselves. Foster this independence and tell your child how proud you are. Point out and celebrate the likes, dislikes, talents, and personality traits that make your child special and lovable.

Awareness of Family and Community

Family is a child's first community. When a child experiences respect and encouragement at home, he or she will enter school ready to contribute based on these same values. As children interact with peers, they begin to understand that others can be similar and different. Encourage your child to accept and respect differences among people, including gender, race, special needs, culture, language, and family structure. Emphasize that in a community, everyone belongs.

Social Relationships and Cooperation

At school, your child will encounter many group activities. He or she will be expected to share materials, take turns, and cooperate with others. To succeed in these situations, your child should know how to be fair, how to compromise, and how to express thoughts and feelings without being overbearing.

4

Helpfulness and Responsibility

Many children ages 4–6 demonstrate the ability to dress themselves, clean up toys, and perform simple household chores. Encourage your child to be increasingly responsible for keeping track of his or her things, and for getting ready for school. Also emphasize to your child the importance of taking responsibility for his or her own behavior. Responsibility includes being honest and trustworthy.

Understanding Emotions and Self-Control

Young children are learning how to handle their emotions, which may tend to the extreme. Focus on helping your child name his or her feelings and express them in appropriate ways. Children will most likely encounter some problems and frustrations at school. You can help your child develop the skills needed to wait patiently, to respect the rules, and to handle disappointment. Habits of self-control will help your child succeed in school and in life.

Focus on: Essential Social Skills

My child is able to:

- **Identify others by name.**

- **Be enthusiastic about going to school.**

- **Listen attentively for three or more minutes.**

- **Try new things, and try them again if the first time fails.**

- **Join conversations.**

- **Play with other children without fighting.**

- **Share toys and other materials.**

- **Recognize authority.**

- **Put away toys and help with chores.**

- **Work independently.**

PLAY AND LEARN
Fun With Social Skills

Tips and Ideas

- Play board games together. Emphasize taking turns, being honest and fair, and practicing good sportsmanship.

- If your child has not had much experience sharing toys and other materials with siblings, provide opportunities where he or she can share items with cousins, friends, or neighbors. Talk about how it feels to share.

- Assign simple household chores for each day or week. These may include making the bed, clearing dishes, sorting socks, or caring for a pet. Praise your child and thank him or her for being so helpful.

- Talk with your child about ways people in your family help each other. Brainstorm what you might do to help others in your city or town. Make a small donation to a local food bank or animal shelter, help with an event at your church or library, or donate some of your child's clothes or toys to a charity. Help your child come up with a plan and carry it out.

Show and Tell

Your child's teacher may plan a regular show-and-tell activity. Give your child some practice by having a show-and-tell time at home, too. Invite each family member to share a meaningful item and tell a story about it. Talk about how each shared item reflects the special characteristics and interests of its owner. Spend some time discussing how it feels to stand and talk in front of others. Praise your child's ability to talk and share with you!

Don't Interrupt!

Waiting to speak can be quite a challenge for the energetic child who wants to share discoveries and ask lots of questions. Explain to your child what interrupting sounds like and looks like. Play a game in which you talk for several minutes about a topic of great interest to your child, such as a favorite movie or an upcoming outing. Praise your child when he or she is able to wait for his or her turn to talk.

Raise Your Hand

Many teachers expect children to raise their hands before they speak in class. Give your child some practice by playing a game during a meal or during a long car ride. Use a sheet of stickers that you know your child will like. Ask your child to raise his or her hand before speaking. Each time, "call" on your child, respond to the comment, and place a sticker on his or her shirt. When your child collects 10 stickers, offer praise or a special treat.

Respect the Rules

Many teachers display a list of classroom rules. Ask your child to share the rules in his or her classroom, or ask the teacher for a copy. Talk about the rules with your child and ask if they are fair and helpful.

Encourage your child to give examples of situations in which the rules were enforced or in which the rules solved a problem. Provide some possible situations, such as "what if someone hit someone else on the playground," and ask your child how the rules might be applied. You may wish to work together to write and illustrate a list of "House Rules" to guide interactions at your home.

Class Rules

1. Listen carefully.
2. Follow directions.
3. Be kind in your words and actions.
4. Take care of your things and the things that belong to our school.

Mr. and Mrs. No-Manners

Share a silly pretend tea party or picnic with your child. Set out a tablecloth and pretend or non-breakable dishes. Tell your child that you are members of the No-Manners family. Ask your child to give the rules for your meal—rules that are the *opposite* of good table manners. For example, your child might say that napkins should go on the floor, that food should be chewed with your mouths open, and that everyone should complain about the food! Have fun pretending to be in the No-Manners family. Then say, "I'm sure glad those rude people don't live at our house!"

Tips and Ideas

- Look through old photos with your child. Share stories from the past and talk about how much your child has grown and how proud you are.

- Help your child make a scrapbook of things to be proud about. It may include certificates, artwork, school papers, photos, and stories. Add to the scrapbook over time, and "read" it from time to time before bed.

- Allow your child to independently select a favorite item at the grocery store, a new T-shirt at the clothing store, or a book at the library. Affirm that your child likes certain foods, colors, characters, and hobbies, and that these things are part of what makes him or her special.

- Start a conversation with your child by saying, "I used to _____, but now I _____." For example, you might say, "I used to hate broccoli, but now I love it." Encourage your child to follow the pattern by telling how he or she has grown and changed.

I'm Growing Up

Help your child select three photos—one of him or her as a baby, one as a toddler, and one taken recently. Have your child glue each photo to a sheet of paper. On a fourth sheet of paper, invite your child to draw a picture of himself or herself as a ten-year-old. Your child may wish to add more drawings of himself or herself as a teenager, an adult, and even a grandparent!

Have your child sequence and staple the pages to make a book. You or your child may wish to write a sentence below each picture. Read the book together, talking about how much your child has grown and how much growing is still to come. Discuss what your child is able to do at each age.

Family Alphabet

Write the alphabet on a large sheet of paper, leaving space after each letter. Alternately, write each letter of the alphabet on a sheet of paper and staple the pages together to make a book. For each letter, write something that begins with that sound and that describes something special about your family. Have family members contribute ideas that relate to favorite hobbies, places, traditions, relatives, physical characteristics, family history, and cultural background. For example, the letter **A** may be for **athletic**, **B** may be for **brown hair**, and **C** may be for **camping**.

Hooray for Being Different!

Read this poem to your child and invite him or her to act it out.

> Hooray for being different!
> How silly it would be
> If I were just like you,
> And you were just like me.
> I'd scratch when you had chickenpox.
> At school, we'd wear each other's socks.
> Your mom would take me to your home.
> My friends would call you on the phone.
> I'd blow your birthday candles out.
> You'd get my gifts! There is no doubt,
> As anyone can plainly see,
> Different is the way to be.

Happy Birthday

Invite your child to make a birthday cake from play dough. If possible, provide a package of real birthday candles to use as decorations. Ask your child to put candles on the cake to represent his or her age last year, this year, and next year.

Talk about birthday wishes your child has had in the past and might have in the future. Provide simple math problems, such as 3 + 6. Ask your child to answer the problem by inserting the appropriate number of candles in the cake. Then, talk about what grade your child will be in at that age, and what experiences he or she is likely to have.

When I Was a Baby

Draw a picture of yourself when you were a baby.

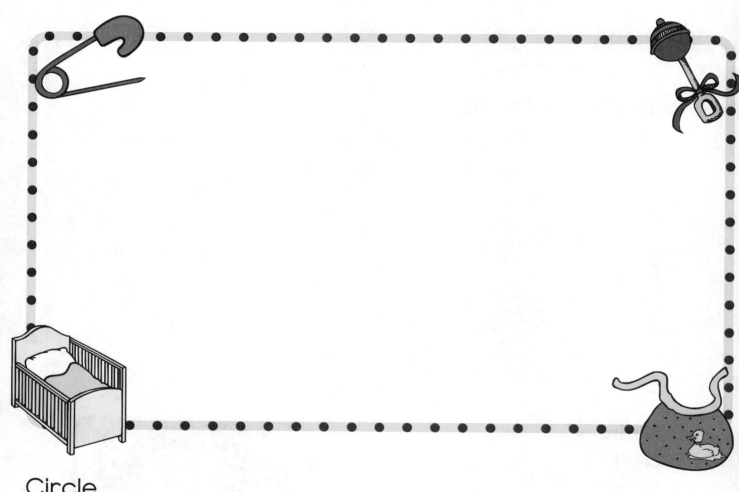

Circle.

I was born on a _____ .

Monday	**Tuesday**	**Wednesday**
Thursday	**Friday**	**Saturday** **Sunday**

I am the _____ child in my family.

only   **first**   **second**   **third**   **fourth**

Social Skills

This Is Me

Draw a picture of yourself. Write your name.

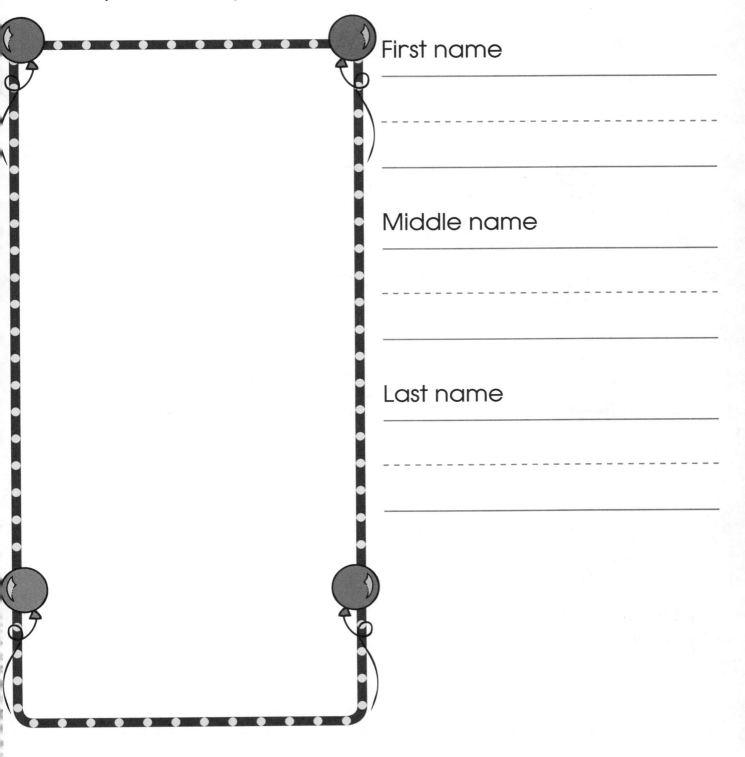

First name

_____

Middle name

_____

Last name

_____

11

Happy Birthday to Me!

Draw candles to show how old you are. Color the cake.

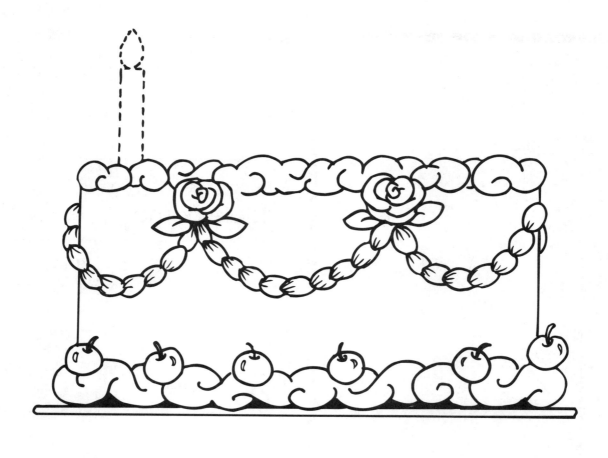

I am _____ years old.

My birthday is

My Favorites

Draw pictures to show your favorite things.

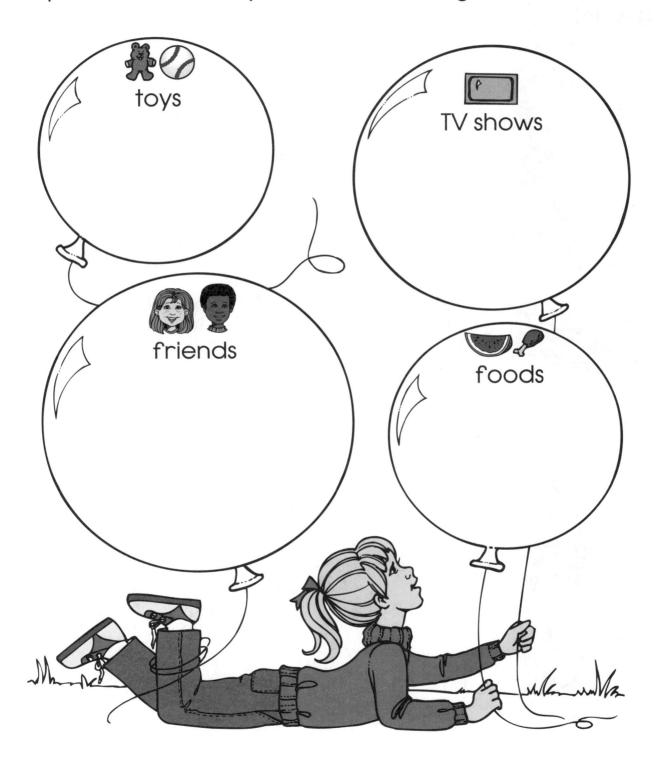

toys

TV shows

friends

foods

So Many Things I Can Do

Color the things that you can do now. Circle the things that you want to learn to do.

When I Grow Up

Color the pictures that show what you might be when you grow up.

Social Skills

When I grow up, I want to be a

_____

- -

_____

My Family Tree

Write the name of each person in your family.

Ask your family to help you!

My Family Tree

Social Skills

This Is My Family

Trace the words. Draw a picture of your family.

father mother

sister brother

My Family Cares for Me

Color the ♡ in each picture that shows how your family loves and cares for each other.

Social Skills

I Share With My Family

Color the pizza. Cut it out and divide it into fair shares for your family.

I Help at Home

Look at the ways you can help at home. Draw a line from each job to the things you would need.

PLAY AND LEARN
All About Friends

Tips and Ideas

- Teach your child how to make simple introductions. Help him or her practice making eye contact and saying, "This is my friend, _____."

- Before a play date, help your child "rehearse" by thinking through what activities the friend might enjoy, what toys will need to be shared, and what problems may arise. Tell your child that he or she knows how to be a good friend!

- Explain to your child that **I** messages are often more effective than **you** messages for solving problems and sharing feelings. For example, say, "I feel sad when you tell me I can't play," instead of, "you're mean when you don't let me play with you."

- Children often work out a number of their problems themselves over time. If you jump in to solve the issues that face your child, you may rob him or her of the opportunity to develop problem-solving skills.

Many Friends

Share this poem with your child.

I have friends both near and far.
Some friends I visit in a car.
Some friends live in my neighborhood.
Having many friends feels good.

All the friends I see at school
Are lots of fun and very cool.
We play with blocks and sand and clay.
I get to see them every day.

I have friends both old and new.
I'm happy that I'm friends with YOU!

We All Share

Point out to your child that everyone shares the air we breathe. Ask, "what else do we all share?" Together, see how many things you can come up with that are shared by everyone. Ask your child to think about sights, sounds, textures, smells, tastes, and feelings that everyone shares.

Sharing Rhyme

Encourage your child to act out this rhyme using two favorite toys.

When I have two toys and you have none
We cannot play, which isn't fun.
So here is what I'm going to do,
I'm going to share my toys with you.
Here's one for you. Now we each have one.
Let's play together. Oh, what fun!

Sweet and Sour

Invite your child to make a face as if he or she has just eaten something sweet. Then, ask him or her to make a face that shows eating something sour. Say these phrases that might be used between friends. Ask your child to make the "sweet" face for kind words and the "sour" face for unkind words.

Good job!	**I don't like you.**
Go away!	**Thank you.**
You are nice.	**You're not in our club.**
Please.	**Come and play.**
You're weird.	**You can't come to my party.**

I'm Sorry

Talk with your child about the importance of apologizing when you've done something wrong. Read this poem together.

It's hard for me to admit
That I've done something wrong.

I wish what I did would go away
So we could get along.

I know that I have hurt you, though.
And the hurt won't go away.

Until I apologize. So I'm ready
To shake your hand and say

I'm sorry.

Friends Are Fun

Look at the friends playing. Write the seasons.

No matter what the weather,
It's fun to play together.
Winter, spring, summer, and fall,
Friendships are the best of all.

spring   fall   winter   summer

My Friends

Draw a picture of two of your friends.

My friends' names are _____

_____

and _____.

We like to _____.

Build-Ups

Build-ups make us feel HAPPY. 😊
Put-downs make us feel SAD. 😞
Put a HAPPY 😊 face by the build-up words.
Put a SAD 😞 face by the put-down words.

Good work!   Let's be friends!

Nice picture!   You can't play.

Go away.   You're nice.

You're smart.   Let's share.

Add a build-up of your own.

_____

- -

_____

Social Skills

Word Power Tower

Cut out the words. Glue on the Power Tower.

| Let's play. | Let's share. | You're great. |
| Hello friend. | Good job. | Thank you. |

Getting Along

Talk about what is happening in each picture. Color the friends who are getting along.

Playing Together

Look at the picture. Point to friends who are having fun together.

Choose one kid in the picture. What do you think the boy or girl is saying to a friend?

32

Friends Are Polite

Look at each picture. Draw lines from the polite sentences to the matching pictures.

Say this if you ask for something.

Say this if your friend gives you something.

Say this if you hurt your friend's feelings.

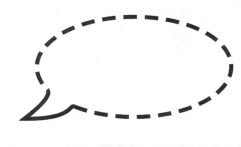

Thank you!   I'm sorry.   Please.

How Should Friends Act?

Draw a line from the center circle to each picture that shows how friends should act. Color the pictures of good friends.

Sharing Feels Good

Count the things that are being shared in each picture.
Write the number in the ☐. Color the pictures.

Tips and Ideas

- As your child grows, he or she learns to be more responsible, or "able to respond" to the larger world. You can help by modeling and encouraging responsible behaviors and by being understanding of mistakes, both yours and your child's.

- Explain to your child that there are some things we have to do, like brushing our teeth, and some things we get to do, like going to a party. Talk about how we all need to keep up with our chores and appreciate our privileges.

- When your child makes a mistake, say, "that's OK." It will be easier for your child to tell the truth and to take responsibility for his or her missteps when they're seen as an expected and accepted part of life.

- When you tell your child to "be good at school," explain what you mean. Encourage your child to listen carefully to the teacher, to follow directions the first time they are given, or to share the balls at recess.

I'm Responsible

Sing this song with your child to the tune of "The Farmer in the Dell."

Oh, I'm responsible.
Oh, I'm responsible.
When I feed my cat
Or hang up my hat
I'm being responsible.

When I'm responsible,
When I'm responsible,
My mom and dad
And teacher are glad,
When I'm responsible.

Two Sides of the Coin

Cover a quarter with masking tape and write **P** on one side and **R** on the other side. Explain that **P** stands for **privilege** and **R** stands for **responsibility**. They are two sides of the same coin. Turn **P** up and say, "It's a privilege to have a pet (or a child, a home, a computer, etc.)." Turn **R** up and say, "It's my responsibility to take care of it." Give the coin to your child and encourage him or her to think of more examples.

A New Job

Ask your child to name a new household chore he or she would like to do. Explain that because your child is getting older, you will teach him or her how to do the job. It may be independently watering the plants, taking out the trash, or using the microwave. Let your child do the job several times, reviewing how well it gets done. Then, celebrate your child's accomplishment with praise and a special treat. Sing this song to the tune of "Are You Sleeping?"

(child's name) can do it.
(child's name) can do it.
Yes, s/he can,
Yes, s/he can.
(child's name) can do (job) now,
(child's name) can do (job) now.
So we say
Hip, hip, hooray!

The Best Policy

It can be hard for young children to distinguish between a lie and the truth. To help your child understand the importance of honesty, share the story "The Boy Who Cried Wolf." Then, ask these questions:
- Did the villagers start out trusting the boy? How do you know?
- Why didn't the villagers help when the boy really needed them?
- Why do you think the boy lied?
- Do you think the boy will lie again?

Spilled Milk

Teach your child the old saying, "Don't cry over spilled milk." Sing this song together to the tune of "London Bridge."

Everybody makes mistakes,
Makes mistakes, makes mistakes.
Everybody makes mistakes,
And that is OK.

Spilled milk isn't worth your tears,
Worth your tears, worth your tears.
Spilled milk isn't worth your tears,
Don't let it spoil your day.

Look What I Can Do

Put a ✓ in the box if you do the activity each day.

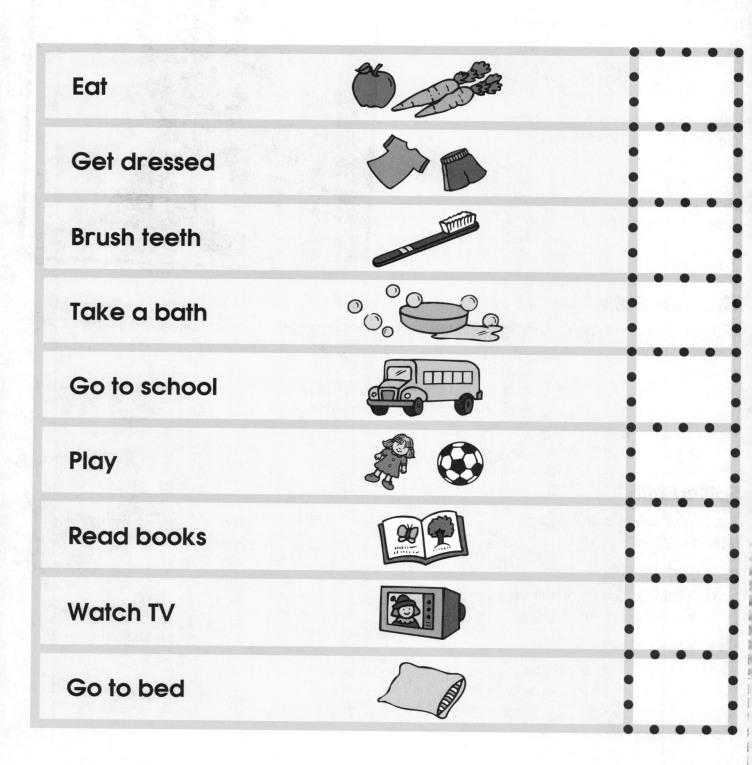

Eat	
Get dressed	
Brush teeth	
Take a bath	
Go to school	
Play	
Read books	
Watch TV	
Go to bed	

Social Skills

I Feel Proud When...

Draw a line to show why each child feels proud.
Color the pictures.

My Jobs

Color the pictures of jobs you do.

Social Skills

When I Am Older

Color the pictures of jobs that you would like to do someday.

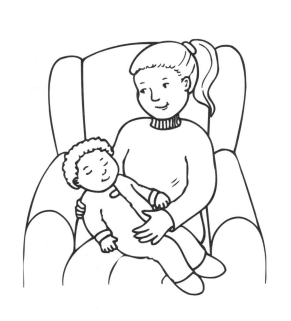

I Can Take Care of Myself

Color each picture that shows how to take good care of your body.

I Can Clean Up

Circle each thing in the bedroom that needs to be cleaned up.

Color the clean bedroom.

What Would I Do?

Read and think about each situation. Put a ✓ in the column that shows what you would do.

	would	would not
Give back a toy I borrowed.		
Call someone a name.		
Make noises at the table.		
Tell an adult about something I lost or broke.		
Blame my friend for something I did.		
Take the biggest piece of cake.		
Throw trash on the floor.		
Send my Grandpa or Grandma a birthday card.		
Say I didn't like a gift I got.		
Ask my friend to lie about something.		
Take a marker from someone's desk.		
Cut in line.		
Help out at home.		
Do my chores without being asked.		
Throw a rock at an animal.		
Tell someone to "get lost."		
Tease and scare my brother or sister.		
Bother the dog when it is asleep.		

Social Skills

Think About It

Talk about what each child is thinking. Color the pictures
that show good choices.

I Can Be Responsible at School

Draw a ☺ in the circle for children who are following the rules at school. Draw a ☹ in the circle for children who are not following the rules.

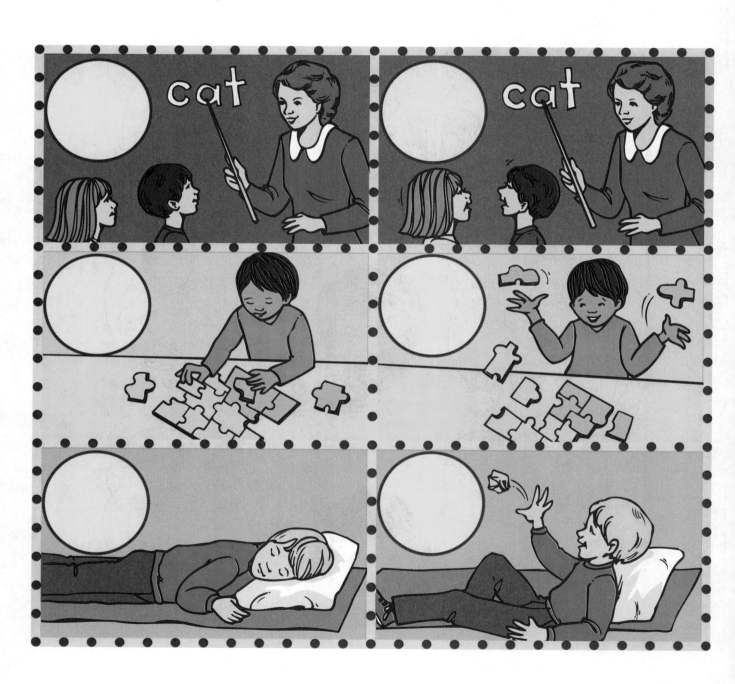

No Excuses

Read what each character said. Write what you would say.

Mom: Did you hang up your wet towel?
Forgetful Felicia: I forgot.
Responsible Rosa: Yes!

You: _____

Teacher: It's time to put away the outdoor toys and come in.
Busy Brady: I'm still playing! Let someone else do it.
Responsible Ross: OK. I'll help.

You: _____

Babysitter: It's time for bed now.
Later Lauren: Later. I don't feel like it right now.
Responsible Rachel: I'll be right there.

You: _____

I Am Honest

Color the picture that shows each boy or girl being honest.

Social Skills

You Can Count on Me

Trace the promises.

You can count on me to . . .

1. Be helpful.

2. Be honest.

3. Be responsible.

PLAY AND LEARN
Feelings and Self-Control

Tips and Ideas

- Teach your child words to identify feelings, including **happy, sad, excited, angry** or **mad, surprised, disappointed, scared, shy, tired, hungry, sick, worried, bored, concerned, pleased,** and **silly.** Encourage your child to use the words to name feelings he or she is experiencing.

- With your child, brainstorm a list of things everyone needs sometimes. Include food, water, sleep, warmth, medicine, comfort, friendship, respect, and love. Help your child practice saying, "I need _____."

- Share with your child what makes you feel safe and comfortable. It may be a cup of something warm to drink, a walk or run, favorite pajamas, or some quiet time to yourself. Ask your child what makes him or her feel safe and comfortable. It may be a favorite toy or blanket, a hug, or a snack. Make a promise to provide these things for each other when you need them.

Body Language

Help your child interpret body language by acting out the following movements. Talk about how each one makes you feel.

- Making the thumbs up sign
- Shaking your finger at someone
- Speaking with hands on hips
- Turning away from a speaker
- Patting someone's arm
- Covering your ears
- Beckoning someone with your fingers
- Holding up your hand like a STOP sign

Everyone Has Feelings

Feelings aren't good or bad, they just are. Name different ways to feel, such as excited, mad, lonely, frustrated, or silly. Ask your child to think of a sound (such as "Yeah!") and an action (such as cheering with hands over the head) to demonstrate each one.

All Better Collage

Talk with your child about things that make us feel better, such as smiles, hugs, compliments, high-fives, jokes, or happy music. Write each thing your child names with a permanent marker on a spare plastic bandage. Invite your child to draw a large sad face on a sheet of paper and to attach the bandage messages all over.

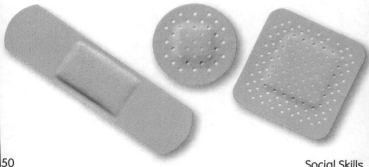

Social Skills

My Motor

Many young children need help with impulse control. Sing this song together to the tune of "Old McDonald Had a Farm."

My motor runs so very slow.
How does my motor go?

I'm sitting still. I am polite.
How does my motor go?

I am relaxed here. I am relaxed there.
I am relaxed here and everywhere I go.

My motor runs so very slow.
How does my motor go?

I'm speeding fast with running feet.
How does my motor go?

I'm grabbing here. I hurry there.
I am speeding here and everywhere I go.

My motor runs like a zooming car.
How does my motor go?

I am the key to my motor.
How does my motor go?

I can slow or speed it up.
How does my motor go?

I make a choice here. I make a choice there.
I make a choice here and everywhere I go.

I am the key to my motor.
How does my motor go?

I Feel Happy

Circle each happy face.

Draw yourself with a happy face.

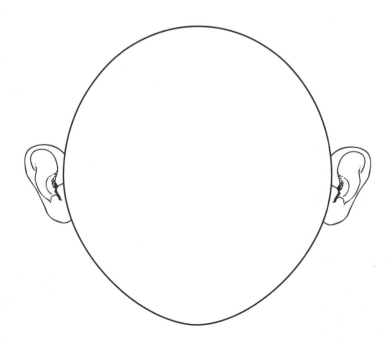

How Do They Feel?

Draw a face to show how each child might feel. Color the pictures.

53

My Feelings

Look at the face beside each mirror. Draw something that might make you feel that way.

How Do I Feel Today?

Cut out the feelings board and the arrow. Clip the arrow to the board. Point the arrow to show how you feel right now.

I Know Words for Feelings

Look at each picture. Write the word that tells how each person feels.

| sad | sleepy | happy | scared |

This girl is _____.

This boy looks _____.

This girl looks _____.

This boy is _____.

Making It Better

Draw a line to show how each sad child can feel better.

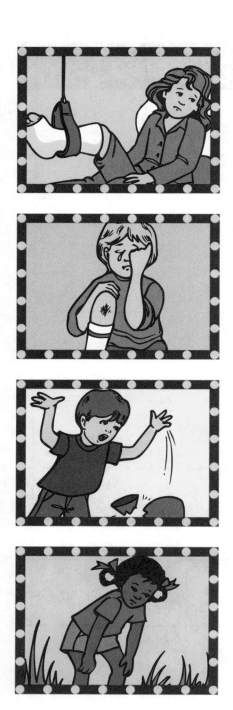

Social Skills

I Get Scared Sometimes

Color the pictures of things that can scare you.

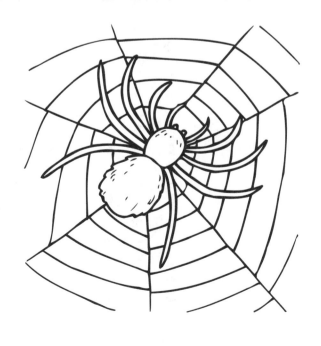

I Like to Feel Safe

Draw a line to show what makes each child feel safe.
Color the pictures.

Sometimes I Need to Move!

Kids can sit or lie still for a while, and then they need to move around! Draw lines from the cow to the children who are mooving.

Time for a Change

It's time to change what the children are doing. Look at the pictures. Draw lines from the children who are moving and playing to picture #1. Draw lines from the children who are sitting to picture #2.

I Can Be a Good Listener

Color the pictures of children who are listening to their parents and teachers. Draw an **X** on the pictures of children who are not being good listeners.

It's Hard to Be Patient

Circle the things that are hardest for you to wait for.

Social Skills

I Am in Control

Cut out and staple the pages to make a little book. Illustrate each page.

3

My impulse to get tough
when I can work it out friendly
is in my control.

2

My impulse to wiggle
when it's time to sit still
is in my control.

_____
(your name)
is in control!

4

My impulse to talk
when it's another's turn
is in my control.

1

I Can Handle This

Saying these things to yourself can help you feel happy and in control. Trace words to complete the sentences.

I have **self control**.

I am **calm**.

I can remember something **funny**.

I will take a deep **breath**.

I can **handle** this.

CUT-APART CARDS
for Fun and Games

Your child can use the cut-apart cards in this book for matching, sorting, playing games, and hands-on learning fun.

Directions

1. Carefully remove pages 69–80 from this book.

2. Cut the cards apart on the dashed lines. You may wish to cover the cards with clear plastic to make them more durable.

3. Store the cards in a zip-top bag.

Card Games and Activities to Play With Your Child

- Match each round Feeling card to a child's expression on another page of this book.

- Choose a triangular Value card. Role-play ways to show that value in action.

- Draw a round Feeling card, but don't show your partner. Make a face showing that feeling. Can your partner guess the emotion?

- Draw a square Situation card. Have each player describe a different way to handle the situation. Discuss and decide on the best approach.

- Spread out all the cards. Draw and read a Situation card. Match it to a Feeling card that tells how the situation would make you feel. Then, choose a Value card and tell how you would apply that value to the situation.

EXCITED

SOMETHING SPECIAL

Tomorrow, your class is going on a special trip. You can hardly wait. You are so excited that it is hard to pay attention to the story your teacher is reading. What would you do?

Social Skills

IT BROKE!

You are playing inside and a ball flies into a lamp. The bulb inside breaks, but the lamp is OK. Maybe your grandma won't notice until she tries to turn on the light. What would you do?

OUT OF PLACE

You go to get a drink from the water fountain at school and you see a pair of sharp scissors on the floor. They don't belong to you. What would you do?

IT'S MINE

You get a new scooter for your birthday. You ride it over and over until you are tired. Your brother, sister, or friend asks for a turn to ride. But it's your new toy. And it's your birthday! What would you do?

SOMEONE NEW

A new boy or girl joins your class at school. He or she asks you to show where the puzzles are kept. But you are busy playing with your friends. What would you do?

LATE !

You don't want to go to school today. When your mom or dad tells you to get ready, you keep playing. Your mom or dad calls you again and says you are going to be late. What would you do?

GOOD AND BAD

Lunch is macaroni and cheese, one of your favorites. But there are also green beans, which you don't like. You know that vegetables are good for you. What would you do?

SOMETHING SPECIAL

Tomorrow, your class is going on a special trip. You can hardly wait. You are so excited that it is hard to pay attention to the story your teacher is reading. What would you do?

ALL DONE ?

You finished a paper at school and you think you did a good job. But your friend says you did part of it wrong. You must not have heard all the teacher's directions. What would you do?

NOT TODAY

Your best friend is going to come over to play after school. You can't stop thinking about all the fun you will have. But when you get to school, your friend is absent. The teacher says he or she is sick. What would you do?

BULLIES

On the playground, two kids tell one of your classmates that only some people are allowed to play on the slide. What would you do?

SOMEONE NEEDS HELP

Your dad feels sick. He is lying down and you notice he hasn't done the things he normally does after work, like hang up his jacket, get the mail, or feed the dog. What would you do?

ACCIDENT

You are outside playing by yourself and you hear thunder. When you start to run inside, you trip and fall. Your knee is bleeding. What would you do?

MAD

HAPPY

EXCITED

SAD

SILLY

UPSET

WORRIED

HURT

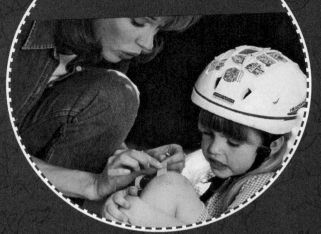

LOVING

SCARED

SURPRISED

SHY

I CAN DO IT!

Be Happy
and Thankful

I CAN DO IT!

Share
With
Friends

I CAN DO IT!

Be Kind
to Others

I CAN DO IT!

Tell
the
Truth

I CAN DO IT!

Be
Helpful

I CAN DO IT!

Keep
Trying

I CAN DO IT!

Take
Responsibility

I CAN DO IT!

Control
My Feelings